EDGE
BOOKS

Revised and Updated

War Planes

Supersonic Fighters
The F-16 Fighting Falcons

by Bill Sweetman

Consultant:
Raymond L. Puffer, PhD, Historian
Air Force Flight Test Center
Edwards Air Force Base, California

Capstone
press

Edge Books are published by Capstone Press,
151 Good Counsel Drive, P.O. Box 669, Mankato, Minnesota 56002.
www.capstonepress.com

Library of Congress Cataloging-in-Publication Data
Sweetman, Bill.
    Supersonic fighters : the F-16 Fighting Falcons / by Bill Sweetman — Rev.
and updated.
        p. cm. — (Edge books. War planes)
    Includes bibliographical references and index.
    ISBN-13: 978-1-4296-1315-6 (hardcover)
    ISBN-10: 1-4296-1315-7 (hardcover)
    1. F-16 (Jet fighter plane) — Juvenile literature. I. Title. II. Series.
UG1242.F5S963 2008
623.74'64 — dc22   2007031329

Summary: Discusses the F-16 Fighting Falcon, its uses, engines, weapons, and future
    in the U.S. Air Force.

Editorial Credits
Matt Doeden, editor; Katy Kudela, revised edition editor and photo researcher;
    Kyle Grenz, revised edition designer

Photo Credits
AFFTC History Office, 4, 9, 10, 13, 16–17, 20
Defense Visual Information Center (DVIC), 7; Capt. Tana R. H. Stevenson, cover
Ted Carlson/Fotodynamics, 1, 7, 18, 22, 24, 27, 29

1 2 3 4 5 6 13 12 11 10 09 08

Table of Contents

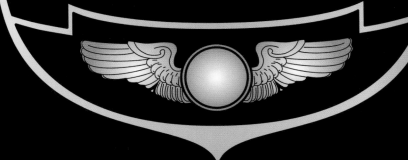

The F-16 in Action

Learn about
- The F-16's mission
- F-16 uses
- F-16 nicknames

It is late at night over Europe. Four U.S. fighter pilots take off from an air base in northern Italy. They are flying Lockheed Martin F-16 Fighting Falcons. Long flames shoot from the planes' jet engines as they climb into the sky.

The pilots fly their planes toward an enemy country. Soldiers from the enemy country are moving tanks and trucks. The enemy soldiers are preparing to attack a neighboring country. The F-16 pilots' mission is to stop the enemy soldiers.

The enemy soldiers stay hidden in the region's many mountain valleys. But the U.S. pilots wear special goggles that help them see at night. The F-16s also have **sensors** that detect the heat given off by the enemy tanks and trucks. These sensors tell the pilots the exact location of the enemy.

One of the pilots points a laser beam at one of the trucks. The light from the laser beam shines a bright spot on the target. The pilot then releases a bomb. The bomb has a sensor that can detect the spot. The bomb hits the first truck in the line. The destroyed truck blocks the road for the other trucks and tanks. The pilots have completed their mission.

sensor — an instrument that detects physical changes in the environment

Building the F-16

Lockheed Martin built the first F-16 in 1976. But this test model was not ready for combat use. The U.S. Air Force did not begin using F-16s until 1979. The Air Force now has more than 1,000 F-16s in service. Each plane costs about $20 million to build.

The United States worked with four other countries to build the first F-16s. The countries were Belgium, Denmark, the Netherlands, and Norway. Each country built different parts of the F-16. Today, F-16s are built entirely in the United States.

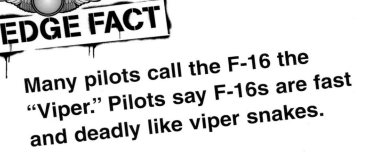

EDGE FACT

Many pilots call the F-16 the "Viper." Pilots say F-16s are fast and deadly like viper snakes.

Print and audio materials charge out for
21 days

DVDs and VHS tapes and console games
charge out for 7 days

SearchOhio allows 3 renewals (if there is
no local hold)

Ohiolink allows 6 renewals (if there is
no local hold)

Fines are $0.50/day

Replacement fee is $25.00 for
lost or damaged materials

Print and audio materials charge out for
21 days

DVDs, VHS tapes and console games
charge out for 7 days

DVDs cannot be renewed

All other items can be renewed once

Fines are $0.50/day

Replacement for lost or
damaged materials is
$20.00 + replacement
cost

Interlibrary Loan Policies

Discover. Learn. Grow.

www.greenelibrary.info

More than 1,000 F-16s have been built since the late 1970s.

About the F-16

The official Air Force nickname for the F-16 is the "Fighting Falcon." The F-16 is one of the world's most successful fighter planes. It allows pilots to perform different missions. Pilots can use the plane as a bomber or a fighter. F-16s are easy to maneuver. Pilots can change the plane's direction and speed quickly. F-16 pilots sometimes perform stunts at air shows to show off the F-16's abilities.

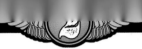

Inside the F-16

Learn about
- F-16 engines
- F-16 controls
- F-16 instruments

The F-16's designers wanted to build a light, easy-to-maneuver combat airplane. The aircraft had to make sharper turns than other fighters. It needed to be able to climb quickly into the air. It had to be able to carry many weapons. The designers also wanted a plane that wouldn't cost a lot to build.

The F-16 is 49 feet, 5 inches (14.8 meters) long. It has a wingspan of 32 feet, 8 inches (9.8 meters). The wingspan is the distance between the tips of the wings. The F-16 is 16 feet (4.8 meters) tall.

Powerful Engine

The F-16 is powered by one jet engine. This engine produces 27,000 pounds (12,150 kilograms) of thrust. The temperature inside the engine can reach 3,000 degrees Fahrenheit (1,650 degrees Celsius). The engine is made of a variety of metals that can withstand these high temperatures.

The F-16's engine gives it a top speed of about 1,500 miles (2,400 kilometers) per hour, twice as fast as the speed of sound. Pilots call this speed Mach 2. Planes that fly at this speed are called supersonic. No airplane can carry enough fuel to fly that fast for long periods of time. F-16 pilots rarely need to fly faster than about 600 miles (965 kilometers) per hour.

The F-16's engine also gives it great climbing power. An F-16 can climb to 40,000 feet (12,000 meters) in about two minutes.

The F-16 can fly at twice the speed of sound.

Climbing this fast creates a great deal of **g-force**. One g is the normal force of gravity on an object that is not moving. The F-16 withstands a g-force of 2.5 when it is climbing. G-forces as high as 9 happen when an F-16 is twisting and turning during battle maneuvers.

g-force — the force of gravity on a moving object

Inside the Cockpit

The F-16 has many controls and some instruments inside its cockpit. Pilots use the controls to fly the planes. Pilots use instruments to keep track of their speed, location, and weapons.

An F-16 pilot's main controls are the control stick, rudder pedals, and **throttle**. Pilots steer their planes with the control stick and rudders. Pilots control their planes' speed with the throttle.

Pilot controls are connected to computers. The computers detect the pilots' commands and make necessary changes to the airplane. For example, a computer releases more fuel into the engine when the pilot pulls the throttle.

throttle — a control on an airplane that allows pilots to increase or decrease the plane's speed

Function:	Multi-role fighter
Manufacturer:	Lockheed Martin
Deployed:	1979
Length:	49 feet, 5 inches (14.8 meters)
Wingspan:	32 feet, 8 inches (9.8 meters)
Height:	16 feet (4.8 meters)
Max. Weight:	37,500 pounds (16,875 kilograms)
Payload:	3,275 pounds (1,485 kilograms)
Engine:	One Pratt and Whitney F100-PW-200/220/229 or one General Electric F110-GE-100/129
Thrust:	27,000 pounds (12,150 kilograms)
Ceiling:	Above 50,000 feet (15 kilometers)
Speed:	1,500 miles (2,400 kilometers) per hour
Range:	2,000 miles (3,200 kilometers)

Most F-16 instruments are in the cockpit's front. The pilot uses a head-up display (HUD) to read the instruments. The pilot can look at the HUD without looking down. All the necessary flight information is available to the pilot in a single location.

AIM-9 missile

AMRAAM missile

bomb

cockpit

tail

engine

bomb

AIM-9 missile

Weapons and Tactics

Learn about

- F-16 missiles
- Dogfights
- Pilots and g-forces

The F-16 is fast and powerful, and its weapons make it deadly. The plane can weigh up to 37,500 pounds (16,875 kilograms) when it is fully loaded. This weight can include bombs, missiles, fuel, and extra electronic equipment.

Each F-16 carries one M61A1 Vulcan cannon built into the left wing. The Vulcan can fire 100 shells per second.

The AGM-88 is one of the F-16's air-to-ground missiles.

Air-to-Air Missiles

The F-16 usually carries AIM-9 Sidewinder air-to-air missiles (AAMs) on its wingtips. The Sidewinder has a heat-seeking device in its nose. This device guides the missile toward the heat from an enemy airplane's exhaust. Jet engines release this heated air as they operate. The Sidewinder has a range of about 10 miles (16 kilometers).

Some Fighting Falcons carry AIM-120 Advanced Medium-Range Air-to-Air Missiles (AMRAAM). AIM-120s are guided by radar. They have a range of about 40 miles (64 kilometers).

Air-to-Ground Weapons

Many F-16s also carry air-to-ground weapons. Pilots use these weapons to attack targets on the ground. Ground targets may include enemy tanks and enemy bases.

Some F-16s carry laser-guided bombs (LGBs). These F-16s carry a device that creates a laser beam. Pilots aim this narrow beam of light at ground targets. Pilots then release the LGBs. The LGBs have sensors that detect the laser. The bombs then head toward the target.

F-16s also carry air-to-ground missiles. The AGM-88 HARM is designed to detect enemy radar on the ground. Enemies may use radar to aim missiles at F-16s. The AGM-88 destroys the enemy's radar. This protects F-16s from enemy missiles.

F-16s sometimes fly in groups called formations.

Combat

F-16 pilots often work in groups to perform missions. They fly in formations. Pilots arrange their formations according to their missions.

F-16 pilots sometimes take part in aerial combat. Pilots sometimes call an aerial battle a "dogfight." Pilots in a dogfight must make sharp turns. They may climb and fall rapidly. They must position their F-16s to fire on enemy planes. They also must avoid enemy attacks. These quick movements can create strong g-forces.

A pilot's body cannot withstand the high g-forces that an F-16 can. Pilots may become unconscious if g-forces are too strong. Their blood flows to the lower parts of the body. The brain does not receive enough blood. Pilots wear G-suits to correct this problem. G-suits squeeze the pilot's lower body and force blood to the pilot's head. G-suits allow pilots to remain conscious at high g-forces.

EDGE FACT

Pilots compress their stomach muscles and do "grunt breathing" to withstand high g-forces.

Serving the Military

Learn about
- Smart bombs
- Improved technology
- The Desert Falcon

The F-16 remains one of the best combat airplanes in the world. But the U.S. military is working to improve the airplane. The military is designing better weapons for the F-16. It also is improving the plane's electrical systems and radar.

New Weapons
The U.S. Air Force is adding new and powerful weapons to its F-16s. These missiles improve pilots' ability to attack ground targets.

The Joint Direct Attack Munition (JDAM) is a new F-16 weapon. Pilots call the JDAM a "smart bomb." The JDAM has a Global Positioning System (GPS) receiver in its tail. Satellites orbiting earth send signals to this device. The signals guide the JDAM to its target. Some F-16s carry the Joint Stand-Off Weapon (JSOW). This bomb is another version of the JDAM.

Future F-16 pilots will wear special helmets that help them aim missiles. The helmets allow pilots to select targets just by looking directly at them. Pilots may use these helmets to aim missiles such as the AIM-9 Sidewinder.

The Desert Falcon

Engineers at Lockheed Martin built a new model of the F-16. It is called the Desert Falcon. The Desert Falcon will carry fuel in two tanks above the plane's body. This extra fuel increases the F-16's range.

The Desert Falcon will include improved sensors. Its radar system will produce clearer images of targets. It also will be better able to track moving targets.

The Desert Falcon will be able to carry improved weapons. It will carry two Black Shaheen missiles under its wings. These jet-powered missiles have a range of more than 200 miles (320 kilometers). The Desert Falcon will carry sensors that will make AGM-88 HARM missiles more effective.

The Desert Falcon will join the Fighting Falcon in air forces around the world. Experts believe the F-16 will remain the world's most important fighter plane until at least 2020.

EDGE FACT

The U.S. military is not the only group to use the F-16. At least 19 nations have the F-16.

GLOSSARY

g-force (JEE FORSS) — the force of gravity on a moving object

laser beam (LAY-zur BEEM) — a narrow, intense beam of light

mission (MISH-uhn) — a military task

radar (RAY-dar) — equipment that uses radio waves to locate and guide objects

rudder (RUHD-ur) — a metal plate attached to a plane to help the pilot steer

sensor (SEN-sur) — an instrument that detects physical changes in the environment

throttle (THROT-uhl) — a control on an airplane that allows pilots to increase or decrease the plane's speed

thrust (THRUHST) — the force created by a jet engine; thrust pushes an airplane forward.

viper (VYE-pur) — a snake that kills its prey with venom; many pilots call the F-16 the "Viper."

READ MORE

Abramson, Andra Serlin. *Fighter Planes Up Close.* New York: Sterling, 2008.

Bledsoe, Karen E. *Fighter Planes: Fearless Fliers.* Mighty Military Machines. Berkeley Heights, N.J.: Enslow, 2006.

Zuehlke, Jeffrey. *Fighter Planes.* Pull Ahead Books. Minneapolis: Lerner, 2006.

INTERNET SITES

FactHound offers a safe, fun way to find Internet sites related to this book. All of the sites on FactHound have been researched by our staff.

Here's how:
1. Visit *www.facthound.com*
2. Choose your grade level.
3. Type in this book ID **1429613157** for age-appropriate sites. You may also browse subjects by clicking on letters, or by clicking on pictures and words.
4. Click on the **Fetch It** button.

FactHound will fetch the best sites for you!

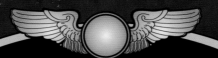

INDEX